FRANKLIN DELANO ROOSEVELT

The Presidents of the United States

George Washington
1789–1797

John Adams
1797–1801

Thomas Jefferson
1801–1809

James Madison
1809–1817

James Monroe
1817–1825

John Quincy Adams
1825–1829

Andrew Jackson
1829–1837

Martin Van Buren
1837–1841

William Henry Harrison
1841

John Tyler
1841–1845

James Polk
1845–1849

Zachary Taylor
1849–1850

Millard Fillmore
1850–1853

Franklin Pierce
1853–1857

James Buchanan
1857–1861

Abraham Lincoln
1861–1865

Andrew Johnson
1865–1869

Ulysses S. Grant
1869–1877

Rutherford B. Hayes
1877–1881

James Garfield
1881

Chester Arthur
1881–1885

Grover Cleveland
1885–1889

Benjamin Harrison
1889–1893

Grover Cleveland
1893–1897

William McKinley
1897–1901

Theodore Roosevelt
1901–1909

William H. Taft
1909–1913

Woodrow Wilson
1913–1921

Warren Harding
1921–1923

Calvin Coolidge
1923–1929

Herbert Hoover
1929–1933

Franklin D. Roosevelt
1933–1945

Harry Truman
1945–1953

Dwight Eisenhower
1953–1961

John F. Kennedy
1961–1963

Lyndon Johnson
1963–1969

Richard Nixon
1969–1974

Gerald Ford
1974–1977

Jimmy Carter
1977–1981

Ronald Reagan
1981–1989

George H. W. Bush
1989–1993

William J. Clinton
1993–2001

George W. Bush
2001–2009

FRANKLIN DELANO ROOSEVELT

DAN ELISH

Marshall Cavendish
Benchmark
New York

Marshall Cavendish Benchmark
99 White Plains Road
Tarrytown, New York 10591-5502
www.marshallcavendish.us

All Internet addresses were correct at the time of printing.

Library of Congress Cataloging-in-Publication Data

Elish, Dan.
Franklin Delano Roosevelt / by Dan Elish
p. cm. — (Presidents and their times)
Summary: "Provides comprehensive information on President Franklin Delano Roosevelt and places him within his historical and cultural context. Also explored are the formative events of his times and how he responded"—Provided by publisher.
Includes bibliographical references and index.
ISBN 978-0-7614-2841-1
1. Roosevelt, Franklin D. (Franklin Delano), 1882–1945—Juvenile literature. 2. Presidents—United States—Biography—Juvenile literature. 3. United States—Politics and government—1933–1945—Juvenile literature. I. Title. II. Series.
E807.E54 2009
973.917092—dc22
[B]
2007025619

Editor: Christine Florie
Publisher: Michelle Bisson
Art Director: Anahid Hamparian
Series Designer: Alex Ferrari

Photo research by Connie Gardner

Cover photo by Hulton Archive/Getty Images

The photographs in this book are used by permission and through the courtesy of: *Corbis*: Oscar White; 3, 28, 85; Bettmann, 6, 20, 22, 26, 33, 35, 36, 39, 41, 44, 45, 47, 48, 66, 68, 77, 79, 80, 82, 86 (R), 87 (L); CORBIS, 8, 10, 12, 17, 18, 28, 31, 49, 73, 74, 76, 86 (L); Hulton Deutsch Collection, 42; Underwood and Underwood, 63; *Getty Images*: Hulton Archive, 9, 38, 65, 69, 87 (R); *The Granger Collection*: 15, 24, 51, 54, 55, 57, 60; *The Image Works*: Topham, 72.

Printed in Malaysia
1 3 5 6 4 2

"If civilization is to survive, we must cultivate the science of human relationships—the ability of all peoples, of all kinds, to live together, in the same world."
—President Franklin Delano Roosevelt

A Youth of Privilege

With the possible exception of Abraham Lincoln, who led the country through the difficult years of the Civil War, no American president has been faced with the challenges of **Democrat** Franklin Delano Roosevelt. From a personal standpoint, there was the **polio** he contracted at age thirty-nine—a disease that left him paralyzed from the waist down. Despite years of effort, Roosevelt spent the latter part of his life largely confined to a wheelchair, unable to walk without the assistance of crutches and heavy, metal braces. Even so, Roosevelt remained active in politics, ultimately leading the country through two of the most severe crises in its history: the Great Depression of the 1930s and World War II. In the process he became one of the most popular and hated men of his day. To America's less fortunate, Roosevelt was a kind father figure who cared deeply about their problems and used the presidency to help "the forgotten man." To many of America's rich, however, Roosevelt was "a traitor to his class," reviled for passing reforms that muted the power of big business and gave relief to America's poor. Refusing to utter his name, Roosevelt's detractors called him "that man in the White House."

Still, by the time he died, at the start of his fourth term, Roosevelt had earned the grudging respect of even many hard-line **Republicans**. After the horrors of World War I (1917–1918), most Americans had no desire to fight another European war. But by the mid-1930s, Roosevelt realized that Germany, Italy, and Japan posed threats that had to be taken very seriously. As Adolf Hitler marched through Europe, Roosevelt did what he could to get the United States involved in the war. After the Japanese bombed Pearl Harbor, a U.S. military base in Hawaii, in 1941, Roosevelt drew on the expertise of Republicans and Democrats alike to prepare the nation and rallied the country to win the war. Like many young men of his era, the former senator Bob Dole of Kansas served in World War II. Though a Republican, Dole called Roosevelt an "energetic and inspiring leader during the dark days of the Depression" and "a tough, single-minded Commander in Chief during World War II, and a statesman."

Today most Americans would agree.

GROWING UP AT HYDE PARK

The young Sara Delano Roosevelt is photographed with her infant son, Franklin, circa 1882.

In the spring of 1880 there was a dinner party in New York City. The hostess was Mrs. Theodore Roosevelt, the mother of the future twenty-sixth president. In attendance were two family friends, twenty-five-year-old Sara Delano and a fifty-one-year-old widower named James Roosevelt. Despite their age difference, James and Sara hit it off. The couple was engaged that summer and married on October 7, 1880, on a beautiful autumn day. A little more than a year later, on January 30, 1882, Franklin Delano Roosevelt was born. In his diary his father called him "a splendid large baby boy. He weighs ten pounds, without clothes."

James Roosevelt was a member of the sixth generation of Roosevelts, who had ultimately settled along New York's Hudson Valley. By the time Franklin was born, James had acquired Springwood, an estate in Hyde Park, New York, with nearly 1,000 acres of land and stunning views of the Catskill Mountains. As the historian Ted Morgan notes, the estates of the upper Hudson Valley of the late

Franklin Delano Roosevelt, age 7

1800s "had more in common with Queen Victoria's England than with the rest of America." Most of the poor in the neighboring villages worked for the estate owners, typically men of leisure who lived off of savings, investments, and family money. As a result, it can be safely said that Franklin Roosevelt grew up in the lap of luxury. When his father traveled to New York City, he rode in a private railroad car. As a boy Franklin played with the children of other millionaires. When he got a haircut, he was brought into town by a governess and told not to speak to anyone.

Franklin's early education was supplied by his mother, who taught him to read and write by age six. After that a series of governesses was employed to tutor young Franklin in Latin, French, German, history, geography, science, and math. Every minute of

James Roosevelt was a prosperous business-man, affording his family a life of luxury. Here he is photographed with young Franklin.

his day was scheduled. There was schooling in the morning, followed by playtime, lunch, then more schooling. While his mother could be strict, his older father, "Popsy," didn't have the stomach for severe discipline. Once, when young Franklin had played a trick on one of his governesses, his mother sent him to his father. James looked up from a book and said, "Consider yourself spanked."

By all accounts, Franklin was a cheerful, good-natured boy who was dominated by a doting mother. "His father and I always expected a great deal of Franklin," she wrote. "After all, he had many advantages that others boys did not have." From the start, Sara was determined to show her son the world. Between ages two to fourteen Franklin made eight trips to Europe, in an era when sea travel was still considered dangerous. Tables on the boats came with "fiddles," or slots where plates and glasses fitted. Chairs were bolted to the floor. Returning to the United States in 1885, the Roosevelts encountered a severe storm that flooded their cabin. Sara wrapped her fur coat around Franklin, declaring, "Poor little boy, if he must go down, he is going down warm."

Another notable event from Franklin's youth occurred a couple of years later, when his parents took him to Washington, D.C., to visit family friends. As it turned out, one of those friends was Grover Cleveland, the ex-governor of New York and the current occupant of the White House. According to legend, Cleveland patted five-year-old Franklin on the head and said, "My little man, I am making a strange wish for you. It is that you may never be president of the United States."

In an era when most well-off families sent their children to boarding school at age twelve, Sara kept Franklin at home until he was fourteen. Finally, she enrolled him in Groton, an eminent boy's prepatory school. On September 15, 1896, Sara and James accompanied Franklin by private railway car to Massachusetts. That week his mother wrote in her diary, "James and I both feel this parting very much."

GROTON AND HARVARD

Groton was founded by Reverend Endicott Peabody, a man both loved and feared by his students. He believed that his boys had an obligation to give something back to their country. "If some Groton boys do not enter political life and do something for our land," he once said, "it won't be because they have not been urged."

Peabody ran a tight ship. At his school the boys were expected to dress for supper in a white shirt and tie. There were early-morning chapel visits and evening prayers. Older boys helped to discipline younger ones. If a younger student was seen to be disobedient, he might be "boot boxed," or crammed into a footlocker. Worse, a boy could be "pumped," his head stuck in a sink, and then water poured over him. It was a punishment so brutal that some victims nearly drowned and had to be resuscitated.

Upon arriving at his first real school, Franklin was at a disadvantage. With most of the other boys already having two years of formal schooling under their belt, Franklin had to throw himself into

While at Groton, Roosevelt (back center) managed the school's baseball team.

every activity in an effort to fit in. Unfortunately, at only 5 feet 3 inches tall and skinny, Franklin wasn't particularly athletic. In his first year he made the seventh-string football team. In baseball he made the Bum Baseball Boys, the worst players in the school. Determined to succeed at something, Franklin finally made his mark in the high kick, a game played only at Groton, in which the player had to leap into the air and kick a tin pan suspended from the ceiling of the gym. Franklin eventually became class champion, reaching 7 feet, 3.5 inches.

Though Franklin was perceived as a bit of a teacher's pet in his first year, by the end of his time at Groton, he had become a class leader. Having grown seven inches, he grew in self-confidence and even worked his way up to the second-string football team. Most important, given his future career, he became a star debater and was well liked around campus. One of his classmates remembered his "most friendly and understanding smile."

Like most Groton graduates, Franklin remained staunchly loyal to his headmaster to the end of his life. When Endicott Peabody died in 1944, Roosevelt wrote, "The whole tone of things is going to be a bit different from now on, for I have leaned on the Rector all these many years far more than most people know."

HARVARD

In the fall of 1900 Franklin followed many of his fellow classmates to Harvard University. Again his family's enormous wealth smoothed his transition to college life. Instead of the dorms in Harvard Yard, Franklin lived off campus in a two-bedroom apartment in the fancy "Gold Coast" neighborhood of Cambridge. He ate at a private dining hall.

As in prep school, Franklin did not make his mark in athletics. At 145 pounds he was too light to play football and not strong enough to row crew. But while he failed in sports, Franklin found his niche as a newspaperman, working as a reporter for the *Harvard Crimson*. During his freshman year, Franklin got a great scoop. His cousin Theodore Roosevelt, then the vice president, was in town. When Franklin called him at his hotel, Theodore said he would be happy to see him the following morning directly after Professor Albert Lowell's nine o'clock class, where Theodore would be lecturing on government. Though the lecture was being kept quiet to avoid big crowds, Franklin printed the news on the front page of the next day's *Crimson*: VICE-PRESIDENT ROOSEVELT TO LECTURE IN GOVERNMENT I THIS MORNING AT 9 IN SANDERS. The lines to see Theodore Roosevelt stretched far out the door. Professor Lowell was furious, but Franklin's scoop helped him win the election as one of the *Crimson*'s five editors.

If Franklin thought that moving to Boston might place some distance between himself and his devoted mother, he was wrong. Sadly, Popsy, his beloved father, died during his freshman year. Though dismayed by the loss, Franklin rebounded quickly by throwing himself into his busy schedule with even more intensity.

But with nothing to keep her at Hyde Park, Sara took it upon herself to move to Boston for the winter months so she could be closer to her son. She even threatened to take classes at Harvard and sit next to Franklin so she could see what he was studying—not that Franklin studied a great deal. Throughout his college career, Franklin was content to earn what was known as

CLUBS OF THE ELITE

In Franklin Roosevelt's era acceptance into a variety of elite clubs and fraternities was essential to ensure a student's social status. To his immense relief, Franklin was elected to the Institute of 1700 during his sophomore year, a club that took about a quarter of his class and often led to memberships in other, more illustrious, clubs. In January of 1902 Franklin was finally asked to join the fraternity Delta Kappa Epsilon, also known as "Dickey." Though thrilled, Franklin knew that acceptance meant a week-long initiation. Every time an upperclassman in the fraternity asked him his name, he was required to answer, "Fool Roosevelt." Other favorite tasks included kissing babies on the street; shouting, "I am passionately fond of animals"; and demanding back money at the end of shows.

Though pleased to be a Delta man, Franklin was ultimately disappointed when he was not asked to enter Porcellian, the most exclusive club of them all. Years later Roosevelt told a friend that his rejection from Porcellian was "the greatest disappointment of my life."

Roosevelt (seated at center) was editor in chief of the Harvard Crimson *during his senior year at Harvard University.*

a "Gentleman's C" and described his time at Harvard as "a little studying, a little riding, a few party calls."

One thing Franklin took absolutely seriously was the newspaper. He wasn't the most talented reporter on staff, but as Franklin himself put it, he "worked like a dog." In the fall of 1902 he was rewarded for his hard work with a promotion to assistant managing editor of the *Crimson*. A friend on the paper described his management style, saying, "In his geniality there was a kind of frictionless command." At the same time, however, another editor thought him "a bumptious, cocky, conceited chap, with a great name but nothing much else." Even so, in his senior year, Franklin won the ultimate prize: he was named editor in chief of the paper, a position that made him one of the leading lights of his class. Later Franklin liked to remind the newsmen covering the White House that he understood the difficulties of their job because he was a reporter, too.

During the summer of 1903, Franklin treated himself to his first trip abroad without his mother. "Don't worry about me," he wrote to her. "I always land on my feet—but wish you were here with me." In truth Franklin was thrilled to be across the Atlantic, able to do whatever he wanted when he wanted. Though he had already finished his required coursework, he returned to Harvard the following fall to edit the *Crimson*. He graduated in the spring of 1904.

A Start
in Politics

*I*n late November of 1903, Sara wrote in her diary, "Franklin gave me quite a startling announcement." That day he had told her of his intention to marry his fifth cousin once removed, Eleanor Roosevelt.

The two cousins had known each other in passing since they were children. In January of 1903 Franklin invited Eleanor to his birthday party at Hyde Park. Over the course of the next months, the couple saw each other at parties in the city and country. Late in the summer Franklin invited Eleanor to visit his family at their home on Campobello Island in New Brunswick, Canada. By the time Franklin was back at school in the fall of 1903, he was in love. At first glance it seemed like an odd match. Franklin was outgoing, self-confident, and fun loving. Eleanor was shy and not considered attractive. As a young girl she was so serious that her mother called her "Granny." Whereas Franklin grew up in a secure household, Eleanor was

Roosevelt married his fifth cousin, Eleanor, in 1905.

A Difficult Childhood

Eleanor Roosevelt was the daughter of Elliot Roosevelt, the younger brother of Theodore, the twenty-sixth president. Though good looking and charming, Elliot had trouble measuring up to his talented older brother. In fact, Elliot himself wrote to his father when he was a teenager, "Oh, father will you ever think me a 'noble boy?' You are quite right about Tede (Theodore) he is one and no mistake a boy I could give a great deal to be like in many respects." As Theodore became more and more successful, Elliot struggled with alcoholism. But despite his weaknesses, Elliot was the one bright light in his daughter Eleanor's life. She wrote, he "dominated my life as long as he lived."

Sadly, Eleanor's mother died when she was eight, and Elliot passed away two years later, leaving Eleanor in the care of her strict grandmother. Luckily, at age fifteen, Eleanor was sent to Allenswood Academy, a boarding school in London where the headmistress, Marie Souvestre, became the main positive influence in her early life. By teaching that women should be valued as much as men, Souvestre became the mother Eleanor never had. Though Eleanor Roosevelt would always feel insecure, she grew to become the most impressive First Lady in the nation's history, a tireless champion for the poor and one of her husband's most trusted advisors.

raised by a disapproving grandmother. A teacher had once written that she was "so intelligent, so charming, so good. *Mais elle n'est pas gaie* [but she is not fun]." But in Eleanor, Franklin saw a woman of great depth and intelligence who was deeply compassionate. On the weekend of November 21, Franklin invited Eleanor to the Harvard-Yale football game and proposed the next day, writing in his diary, "After lunch I have a never to be forgotten walk to the river with my darling."

At first Sara tried to delay the marriage. In February of 1904 she took her son and a friend on a five-week Caribbean cruise. Later she tried to get Franklin a job as the secretary of the U.S. ambassador to London. But soon enough Sara realized that delaying or stopping the marriage was a lost cause. "Of course dear child," she wrote her son, "I do rejoice in your happiness, and shall not put any stones or straws ever in the way of it." On March 17, 1905, the couple was married by Endicott Peabody, Franklin's Groton headmaster. The bride was given away by her uncle, Theodore Roosevelt, then the president of the United States.

That summer the couple went on a three-month European honeymoon.

THE STATE SENATOR

After college Roosevelt entered Columbia Law School in New York City, passed the bar exam in the spring of 1907, and took a job at the Wall Street firm Carter, Ledyard and Millburn. On the home front, a first child, Anna, had arrived in May of 1906. James followed a year later. The first Franklin Jr. was born in 1909, but died in infancy. Elliot came in 1910 and the second Franklin Jr. in 1914. Finally, John was born in 1916.

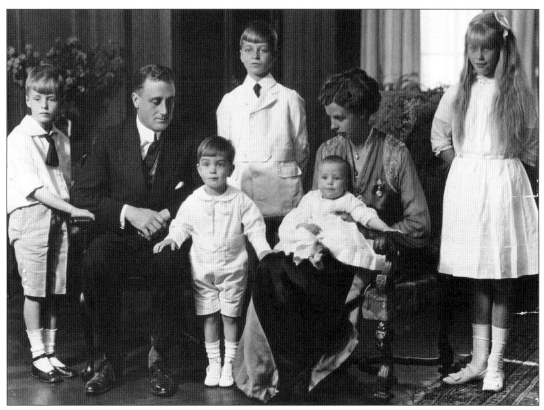

Franklin and Eleanor Roosevelt had six children. One died in infancy.

By all standards, Roosevelt was well on his way to living the kind of comfortable, secure life that most people dream about. From investments and trusts, Franklin and Eleanor had an annual income of $12,000 between them, a huge amount in an era when an average worker earned around $500 a year. Further, in the fall of 1908, his mother had bought adjoining townhouses on East Sixty-fifth Street—one for Franklin and his family and one for her.

But Franklin was quite open about his political aspirations. Grenville Clarke, a college friend and fellow clerk at Carter, Ledyard and Millburn, remembered,

I remember him saying with surprising frankness that he wasn't going to practice law forever and that he wanted to be and thought he had a real chance to be President. I remember that he described very accurately the steps which he thought could lead to this goal. . . . I do not recall that even then, in 1907, any of us deprecated this ambition or even smiled at it as we might perhaps have done. It seemed proper and sincere and moreover, as he put it, entirely reasonable.

By 1910 Roosevelt had come to the attention of Edward E. Perkins, the chairman of Dutchess County, a man on the lookout for Democratic Party talent. First, Perkins asked Roosevelt if he wanted to run for a seat in the state assembly. When Lewis Chandler, the current assemblyman who had not been planning to run for reelection, heard that someone so young was being groomed to succeed him, he decided to run again himself. Undeterred, Perkins suggested that Roosevelt throw his hat in the ring for the state senate for the 26th District instead, a 90-mile tract of land comprising Dutchess, Putnam, and Columbia counties, which ran up the Hudson River. Though excited finally to be getting his start in politics, Roosevelt knew that the odds were against him. For starters, the district almost always voted Republican. Worse, Roosevelt's opponent would be John F. Schlosser, a well-liked lawyer who had already served one term.

Roosevelt realized that his only chance at winning was by meeting as many voters as possible. To do that, he rented a red Maxwell touring car with no top. Traveling the district on dirt roads, he was often forced to stop to let horse teams trot by. But in the end, his efforts paid off. Stopping in every village he passed, Roosevelt gave speech after speech. While he seemed "high strung and nervous" at first (according to Eleanor), over time

Roosevelt addresses his supporters during his 1910 campaign for New York state senator.

Roosevelt was chatting easily with local farmers, addressing crowds as "my friends." On election day, he won by a little over one thousand votes.

In Albany, New York's state capital, Roosevelt had big shoes to fill. Thirty years earlier, cousin Teddy had made a name for himself as a young assembly-man by taking on the most powerful men in his own party. Now many people were looking curiously at Franklin Roosevelt, wondering whether he would try to make a name for himself in a similar fashion. "Big Tim" Sullivan, the boss of **Tammany Hall**, the corrupt Democratic Party organization that unfairly held most of the power over granting government contracts and jobs in the state, was worried, saying, "We'd better take him [Roosevelt] down and drop him off the dock."

In truth Big Tim Sullivan and other Democratic stalwarts were right to be nervous. Shortly after settling in Albany, Roosevelt found an issue to sink his teeth into. At the time U.S. senators were not elected by popular vote but by state legislatures. Holding a majority of seats in the congress, the Democrats were certain to elect whomever they wanted. Big Tim Sullivan and the Tammany organization were backing

William F. Sheehan. Known as "Blue-eyed Billy," Sheehan was a lawyer who was loyal to Tammany Hall. The other candidate was Edward M. Shepard, a lawyer for the Pennsylvania Railroad, who stood for honesty in government. Roosevelt wrote in his diary, "There is no question that the Democratic Party is on trial." Feeling strongly that Shepard was the better candidate, Roosevelt and a group of twenty other Democrats purposefully did not show up in the congress at the time of the vote, keeping Sheehan from amassing the number of votes he needed to secure election. As Roosevelt's later political mentor Louis Howe, then a reporter for the *New York Herald*, wrote at the time, "Never in the history of Albany have 21 men threatened such ruin of machine plans. It is the most humanly interesting political fight of many years." Due to his wealth and family name, Roosevelt was identified as the group's leader in the papers. "There is nothing I love as much as a good fight," he told the *New York Times* in late January. "I never had as much fun in my life as I am having right now."

Yes, Roosevelt was having fun, but more experienced Democrats thought he was being self-defeating. Wasn't the goal to elect a Democrat to the U.S. Senate? Was Shepard really that much better than Sheehan? The future New York governor Al Smith went so far as to call Roosevelt "a damned fool." But in the end Roosevelt held fast until a compromise candidate was found. In an era when Tammany Hall was viewed across the country as a corrupt machine, Roosevelt was heralded as a hero. Papers around the country dubbed him a rising leader of the Democratic Party.

Given his principled first few months in the state senate, Roosevelt was poised to become a party leader on many pressing issues

During the early 1900s, many workers were employed at businesses with horrible conditions and no regulations.

of the day. In the late 1800s, the United States had become an industrial nation. Businesses operated with virtually no government regulation. Therefore, companies could employ women and children for little pay in factories with conditions so terrible, they were called **sweatshops**. On March 25, 1911, a horrific fire swept through the Triangle Shirtwaist Company in New York City. With no working fire escapes, 147 people were killed. However, while Roosevelt scored political points criticizing Tammany Hall, it was the Tammany politicians Robert Wagner and Al Smith who passed laws aimed at improving working conditions. Though Roosevelt eventually became the most important supporter of the poor and working class in the nation's history, in his early career he was sometimes occupied with more trivial issues. When his fellow state senators were trying to make a fifty-four-hour work week for women and children state law, Roosevelt was trying to get votes for a bill that would lower fees for shad fisherman to $5. Frances Perkins, a leading reformer of the day and later Roosevelt's secretary of labor, said,

I have a vivid picture of him operating on the floor of the Senate, tall and slender . . . rarely smiling, with an unfortunate habit—so

natural that he was unaware of it—of throwing his head up. This, combined with his pince-nez [eyeglasses] and great height, gave him the appearance of looking down his nose at most people.

Some historians argue that the conservative region he represented made Roosevelt wary about becoming the vocal advocate of social change he wanted to be. But despite the less progressive views of his **constituents**, Roosevelt did end up voting for most of the more liberal legislation that came before the state legislature. He supported the direct election of U.S. senators and came out in favor of workmen's compensation. After opposing the fifty-four-hour workweek, Roosevelt took to the senate floor and talked about birds until none other than Big Tim Sullivan himself could be roused from bed to cast a deciding vote!

In 1912 Roosevelt was reelected to the state senate. But barely a few months into his term, the new Democratic president, Woodrow Wilson, offered him a dream job: the assistant secretary of the navy.

ASSISTANT SECRETARY OF THE NAVY

Once more, Franklin Roosevelt was following in the footsteps of his famous cousin. Theodore Roosevelt had served as the assistant secretary of the navy before leaving the post in 1898 to fight in the Spanish-American War.

Though only thirty-one years old and a good twenty or thirty years younger than many of the admirals he had been assigned to supervise, Roosevelt wasn't fazed. "I get my fingers into everything," he said, "and there's no law against it." With his boss, the southerner Josephus Daniels, Roosevelt oversaw a navy and marine corps of 65,000 men and an annual budget of

The Loyal Assistant

Louis Howe was not well liked. He was not attractive. He described himself as "one of the four ugliest men . . . in the State of New York." He smoked like a chimney and drank. But he became Franklin Roosevelt's most trusted advisor.

As a newspaperman, Howe had started a grassroots organization to fight Tammany Hall. When Roosevelt was running for reelection to the state senate in 1912, he became so ill that he couldn't get out of bed. Desperate, Roosevelt asked Howe to run his campaign. Howe did such a good job that Roosevelt won without making a single campaign appearance. From that point until Howe's death, in 1936, the promotion of Roosevelt's career became Howe's obsession. James P. Warburg, who would become one of Roosevelt's economic advisors, said,

> I loathed Louis Howe. . . . He always came up with the really cynical political twist to an idea. . . . . But I don't think Roosevelt would have been nearly as a good a politician without Louis Howe. . . . He had very great political intuition.

$150 million. Daily issues included anything from awarding contracts to shipbuilders to meeting with congressional committees or even the president.

Less than a year into the job, he wrote to Eleanor,

A most interesting day. . . . I was suddenly called on by the President to make all the arrangements for sending surgeons, attendants, supplies etc. out to the flood district in Ohio—I had a hectic time getting the machinery going, but the force leaves tonight and I had some interesting work with the Sec. Of War and Gen'l Wood [the Army Chief of Staff].

Roosevelt loved the pomp of the job. Whenever he inspected a ship, he received a seventeen-gun salute—four more guns than admirals with thirty years' service—and a sixteen-man guard standing at attention.

By all accounts, Roosevelt performed his duties well. When war broke out in Europe, in 1914, he testified before Congress that the country needed to build up its defenses and made sure that all navy plants and bases had whatever supplies they needed. When the United States finally joined the war in 1917, Roosevelt threw himself into the task of preparing the navy for action, eventually increasing the number of U.S. commissioned ships from 197 to 2,003. In so doing Roosevelt saw firsthand the epic commitment it took from all agencies of the government to fight a war. He also learned the importance of keeping an open mind when creating policy. Called by one of his admirals "a great trial and error guy," Roosevelt was not a man who stubbornly attached himself to a single solution to a problem. If something didn't work, he gladly chucked the idea and tried another.

During the summer of 1919, with the war won, Roosevelt attended the Paris Peace Conference in France. By that point President Wilson had thrown the weight of his reputation behind creating the **League of Nations**, an international governing

The launching of the U.S.S. Tennessee *at the Brooklyn, New York, navy yard was presided over by assistant secretary of the navy Franklin Delano Roosevelt.*

body that he hoped would maintain world peace. The members of the league would attempt to settle disputes peacefully, through negotiation and diplomacy. But as good as the idea seemed to Roosevelt, many Americans didn't want their fate tied up with that of Europe. So despite the fact that the U.S. president was instrumental in creating the league, the United States never joined it. The U.S. Senate voted against America's entry into the league. It would take until after World War II, with the formation of the **United Nations**, for the nation to join an international organization committed to influencing world events.

RUNNING FOR VICE PRESIDENT

As the presidential race of 1920 shaped up, it looked like it was going to be a bad year for the Democrats. Yes, Woodrow Wilson had been a good president, but eight years of reform and war had made the country ready for a change. That year the Republicans nominated the likable Ohio senator Warren G. Harding, who opposed the nation's membership in the League of Nations and promised voters "a return to normalcy."

While the Republicans were united in their desire to return to simpler, easier days, the Democrats were divided. Some supported joining the League of Nations; some were against it. In the end the party nominated the Ohio governor James M. Cox to run for president. When looking for a running mate, Cox thought instantly of the young, well-spoken assistant secretary of the navy. That Franklin Roosevelt was the cousin of one of the most popular presidents in history didn't hurt. But most important of all, Cox liked that Roosevelt was from New York, a state he desperately needed to carry if he had any hope of winning.

Governor James Cox (left) and Roosevelt campaign during the 1920 presidential election.

In those days vice-presidential candidates didn't generally go out on the campaign trail. But Roosevelt stormed through the country in a special railway car, campaigning in thirty-two states, giving speech after speech in favor of joining the League of Nations. In the end Warren Harding and his running mate, Calvin Coolidge, cruised to an easy victory, winning 61 percent of the vote. In defeat Roosevelt wasn't particularly upset and claimed to be looking forward to taking a break from politics. He wrote to a friend before a well-deserved vacation, "Washington this year will be quite disgusting to live in, and I am thankful that I am to be back in New York trying to practice law and make up for a government salary all these years."

YEARS OF RECOVERY

Three

*I*n the early twentieth century, polio was one of the most dreaded diseases in the United States. An illness that usually struck children, polio left some of its victims paralyzed. Though little was known at the time about how it was contracted (the virus was discovered in 1908, but its route of transmission was not determined for many years), it wasn't unusual for parents to hustle their children out of town when cases arose in a certain area. In 1916, when an epidemic swept through Washington, D.C., Roosevelt hurriedly sent his children and Eleanor to his family estate at Campobello Island in New Brunswick, Canada, where he thought they would be safe. Ironically, it was on the same island that Roosevelt was to be struck with the disease himself.

After the presidential race of 1920, Roosevelt returned to New York, formed a law partnership, and also took a job at Fidelity and Deposit, a bond firm. At the same time he kept involved with the Democratic Party, waiting for his next move back into politics. During the summer of 1921, Roosevelt traveled to Campobello Island for a vacation. On August 10 he spent the day sailing with his children. On the way back they put out a brush fire on a small island, then went for a dip in a freshwater lagoon before trotting home down a 2-mile dirt road in wet bathing suits. Finally, Roosevelt took a dip in the ice-cold Bay of Fundy. As he sat on his porch to read the day's newspapers, Roosevelt didn't feel well and went to bed without eating dinner.

LUCY MERCER

In 1918 Eleanor Roosevelt made a horrible discovery: Franklin was in love with another woman, Lucy Mercer, who had worked as Eleanor's social secretary before joining the Department of the Navy. In those days divorce was career suicide for a politician. Despite Eleanor's deep hurt and Franklin's sincere love for Lucy, the couple decided to stay together. Their son Elliot said, "It was Louis Howe going back and forth and just reasoning, convincing father that he had no political future if he did this. . . . He convinced her [Eleanor] . . . she could not destroy Franklin's goal and he convinced her that she too would have a great role to play."

From that point forward, Franklin and Eleanor's marriage became more of a political partnership. Though not romantically linked to Eleanor, Franklin still respected his wife enormously. "It became a very close and very intimate partnership of great affection . . . in a tremendously mental sense," Elliot said.

Despite her husband's affair, Eleanor remained one of Franklin's most important confidantes.

The next morning his left leg was numb. He had a temperature of 102 degrees Fahrenheit. A doctor diagnosed the illness as a cold. Just as Franklin Roosevelt hoped his left leg would improve, his right leg gave out, too. By that time Eleanor was sleeping on a mattress on his bedroom floor so she could be on call all day and night. By August 12 Roosevelt couldn't move his legs at all and was so weak, he could barely hold a pen. Another doctor diagnosed a blood clot in the lower spinal cord. It wasn't until almost two weeks later that a third doctor gave the correct diagnosis. Roosevelt had contracted polio.

A NEW LIFE

As days turned into weeks, Roosevelt's condition didn't improve. Still, he struggled to keep up his spirits, joking with his children. James remembered, "He grinned at us, and he did his best to call out . . . some cheery response to our . . . just-this-side-of-tears greetings." Though initially depressed, Roosevelt soon grew determined: he would do whatever it took to walk again. But the odds were against him. By September he was in a hospital in New York City. Dr. George Draper, his doctor, wrote,

> *I feel so strongly after watching him now for over a week that the psychological factor in his management is paramount. He has such courage, such ambition, and yet at the same time such an extraordinarily sensitive emotional mechanism that it will take all the skill which we can muster to lead him successfully to a recognition of what he really faces without utterly crushing him.*

Roosevelt stayed in the hospital through the end of October and continued his convalescence at his home in the city—a

WARM SPRINGS

Once, Eleanor was asked if her husband's illness had changed his character. She replied, "The answer is yes. Anyone who has gone through great suffering is bound to have a greater sympathy and understanding of the problems of mankind."

Nearly all of his friends and colleagues noticed the change. Frances Perkins, who had once complained of Roosevelt's slightly arrogant attitude when he had been a state senator, came to praise his "deeper philosophy." "Having been to the depths of trouble," she said, "he understood the problems of people in trouble."

(continued)

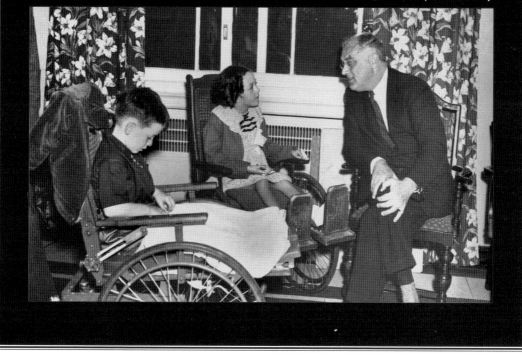

As president, Roosevelt became known for looking out for America's poor. Before he entered the White House, he did what he could for less fortunate polio victims. In the autumn of 1924 Roosevelt first visited Warm Springs, a resort in Georgia where the warm mineral waters of the swimming pool were said to help people with polio. In 1926 Roosevelt bought the resort and turned it into an international center for the treatment of polio victims. Roosevelt became so knowledgeable about the disease that the other patients called him "Dr. Roosevelt."

time that Eleanor described as "the most trying period of my life." Not only was her husband seriously ill, but she and her mother-in-law were arguing bitterly over Roosevelt's treatment and future.

In June Roosevelt moved back to Hyde Park. Fitted with heavy, metal leg braces, he practiced walking, always slowly and painfully, up and down his long driveway. In the fall of 1922, he felt well enough to go back to work at Fidelity and Deposit. Gripping his crutches, he would slowly make his way through the lobby up to his office.

The question remained whether Roosevelt would get back into politics. His mother thought her son should retire to Hyde Park. But Eleanor and Louis Howe encouraged Roosevelt to lead a more active life. In 1924 he made his first public appearance since his illness. At that year's Democratic presidential convention he made a speech on behalf of Al Smith's candidacy. Leaning heavily on his sixteen-year-old son, Jimmy, Roosevelt struggled to the speaker's platform. At the last second he cast his crutches aside and gripped the podium. Calling Smith the "happy warrior of the political battlefield," his oration brought the crowd to its feet, cheering.

Still, Roosevelt remained convinced that he needed to focus on regaining the use of his legs before he could consider running for office again. In 1925 he wrote to his friend Louis Wehle,

I must give principal consideration for at least two years more to getting back the use of my legs. I . . . hope, within a year, to be walking without the braces, with the further hope of then discarding the crutches in favor of canes and eventually possibly getting rid of the latter also.

But Roosevelt would remain paralyzed for the rest of his life. Luckily, other members of the Democratic Party didn't feel that the ability to walk was an absolute prerequisite for higher office. In 1928 the New Yorker Al Smith finally received the Democratic nomination for president. To have an outside shot at winning, Smith felt that he needed to carry his home state of New York. To do that he hoped that having a strong Democratic candidate for governor would compel people to vote for him.

Roosevelt had hopes for walking again without the aid of leg braces and crutches.

Roosevelt posed for this photo the day he learned of his nomination for governor of New York.

There was only one New Yorker who fit the bill: Franklin Roosevelt.

At first Roosevelt refused. He wanted to spend another year trying to regain the use of his legs. Further, Louis Howe advised against it, arguing that 1928 would be a Republican year and that Roosevelt would be likely to lose. In the end Roosevelt couldn't turn down the entreaties of his party. "Well, I've got to run for governor," he told his secretary. "There's no use in all of us getting sick about it!"

To diffuse his poor health as a campaign issue, Roosevelt toured the entire state, logging a total of 1,300 miles in a single month. On the morning of November 6, Roosevelt voted in Hyde Park, then waited for the results. As the votes were counted, it became clear that Al Smith was losing in New York. But the governor's race was too close to call. By the next morning Roosevelt had inched ahead, winning by 25,000 votes out of the 4,200,000 cast. Roosevelt laughed and called himself "the one and a half percent governor."

ONTO THE WHITE HOUSE

Roosevelt found that he loved being back in politics. His first goal was to get control of the way the state spent money. Under previous governors a practice had emerged in which the legislature took on the right of approving how state money was spent. But

Roosevelt thought the powers of the state purse belonged to the governor and reveled in what he called "one continuous glorious fight with the Republican legislative leaders." Early in his term a court handed Roosevelt a victory, ruling that he was right.

As governor Roosevelt began to work for the rights of what he later called "the forgotten man." In July of 1929, 1,300 inmates at Clinton State Prison (otherwise known as the "Siberia of New York") rioted. Six days later, 1,700 inmates in an overcrowded prison in Auburn did the same, leaving two dead and eleven wounded. In response Roosevelt changed some of the state's harsher mandatory sentencing laws, then built a new prison in Attica, New York. Roosevelt also paid attention to the rights of labor, giving workers the right to choose their own doctors and eventually becoming the first governor to favor state unemployment insurance. A popular governor, he was reelected in 1930 by 725,000 votes, the largest plurality in state history.

By that point the United States was suffering the worst economic crisis of its history. In late 1929, after a decade of high living, the stock market crashed. Overnight many Americans lost all the money they had, and the country was plunged into the worst economic crisis in history. The causes were complex. During the 1920s American factories were turning out goods at record rates. But many average American workers did not earn enough money to pay for those goods. In 1929 economists speculated that a typical American family would need an income of $2,000 a year to survive—an amount that only 40 percent of the families in the country earned. Worse, many poor people bought what they needed on credit. At the same time rich investors bid up the prices of stocks well beyond what they were worth. They also bought stocks on credit. When European investors began to

The October 24, 1920, headline of the Brooklyn Daily Eagle *announces the stock market crash.*

withdraw their investments from the United States, a wave of fear swept through the stock market. Soon everyone was trying to sell off stocks and get their money out. On October 24, 1929, thirteen million shares of stock were sold off. The following Tuesday, sixteen million more were sold. Overnight, huge numbers of people went bankrupt. Over the next three years, five thousand banks failed, and a good portion of the wealth of the country simply disappeared.

With more than fifteen million Americans out of work, companies bankrupt, and banks failing, the country looked to President Herbert Hoover for relief. But Hoover felt it was best to let the economic situation turn around on its own. Eventually, under great pressure, he set up the Reconstruction Finance Corporation, a government agency that loaned money to railroads and banks. Americans were outraged. How could the president lend money to businesses while ignoring the poor? In 1932 a crowd of unemployed veterans marched on Washington and had to be chased away by the army. Meanwhile unemployed and homeless Americans lived in makeshift villages that were dubbed "Hoovervilles."

Many of the homeless and unemployed lived in this Hooverville in Seattle, Washington during the Great Depression.

In contrast to Herbert Hoover, Roosevelt was willing to use government money to aid the poor. In 1931 the New York legislature approved an expenditure of $20 million, funded by an increase in the state **income tax**, to form the Temporary Emergency Relief Administration, an organization set up to create jobs for the state's unemployed. Roosevelt said, "It is clear to me that it is the duty of those who have benefited by our industrial and economic system to come to the front in such a grave emergency and assist in relieving those who under the same industrial and economic order are the losers and sufferers."

As the first in the country that provided relief to the poor, Roosevelt's bill attracted national attention. With Hoover out of touch with the national mood, Americans were looking toward the next presidential election. As the governor who had taken action to relieve the suffering people in his state, Roosevelt quickly emerged as a leading candidate. In 1932 the Democratic convention was held in Chicago. With Louis Howe working behind the scenes, Roosevelt won the nomination. In those days nominees never addressed conventions in person. Breaking with precedent Roosevelt flew to Chicago to show the country that he could still be a forceful leader, despite his handicap. "I pledge to you, I pledge to myself, a new deal for the American people," he told the cheering crowd. At the time Roosevelt wasn't sure himself exactly what that meant. In fact, as Roosevelt campaigned across the country, he was purposefully vague on what he intended to do to address the Depression once he was in office. Walter Lippman, a well-known journalist of the day, famously wrote, "Franklin D. Roosevelt is no crusader. He is no tribune of the people. He is no enemy of entrenched privilege. He is a pleasant man, who, without any important qualifications for the office, would very much like to be President."

Roosevelt meets with working-class America in 1932.

Like many Americans, Lippmann overlooked Roosevelt's record as governor. But whether people had faith in Roosevelt or not, Herbert Hoover was so unpopular that it was dangerous for him to campaign. At a campaign stop in Detroit, mounted police had to be called in to disperse a mob.

On election day Americans voted for change. Roosevelt carried forty-two states and won the **Electoral College**, 472 to 59. The man who had been stricken with polio only eleven years earlier was the thirty-second president of the United States.

*T*oday newly elected governors, legislators, and presidents take office on January 20. In 1933 political succession occurred on March 4. As a result Roosevelt had to wait four long months to move into the White House. During that time the Depression worsened.

Unemployment rose. Farmers burned the crops they couldn't sell. Banks failed by the hundreds as worried Americans withdrew their savings. By early March 1933 the U.S. economy had all but shut down. The New York Stock Exchange had closed its doors, as had the Chicago Board of Trade.

Franklin Delano Roosevelt takes the oath of office on March 4, 1933.

Then came inauguration day. On March 4, at noon, Franklin Delano Roosevelt took the oath of office on his family Bible. Facing a cold wind with no hat, Roosevelt reassured the nation, "First of all, let me assert my firm belief that the only thing we have to fear is fear itself, nameless, unreasoning, un-justified terror which paralyzes needed efforts to convert retreat into advance." After more than three years of pessimism and limited action from the White House, Roosevelt's optimism blew across the country like a breath of fresh air. Millions of Americans listening on the radio found hope. One aide said, "Well, he's taken the ship of state and turned it right around."

Over the next one hundred days, Roosevelt introduced a flurry of bills to Congress that aimed to reform the country's broken economic system and provide relief to American's poor. Roosevelt's legislative agenda was soon named after the phrase he had used while accepting the Democratic nomination: the New Deal.

THE BANKING CRISIS

In his inaugural address Roosevelt made it plain that he intended to act decisively to combat the nation's problems. "I shall ask Congress," he said, "for . . . broad **executive power** to wage a war against the emergency, as great as the power that would be given to me if we were in fact invaded by a foreign foe."

Roosevelt was true to his word. The next day, Sunday, March 5, his cabinet met all day. The next morning Roosevelt called for a four-day "bank holiday." Overnight, every bank in the country was closed, and Americans had to rely on the money in their wallets to buy what they needed. Then Roosevelt called for a special session of Congress to convene on March 9. On that day congressmen and senators were handed the **Emergency Banking Relief Act**, a bill that had been drawn up so quickly that the only copy of it was read aloud to the gathered law-makers by a clerk. When majority floor leader Joseph W. Byrns Jr. formally introduced the bill, he asked that the total debate time on it be limited to a mere forty minutes. The law gave the president broad powers to reform America's banking industry.

When banks closed in 1933, teachers in Grosse Point, Michigan, were paid with food.

But Republicans didn't object. "The house is burning down," the minority floor leader said. "And the President of the United States says this is the way to put out the fire."

With the bill in the hands of Congress, Roosevelt turned to selling his banking reform to the American people. Calvin Coolidge and Herbert Hoover, America's two previous presidents, had had a contentious relationship with the press. Hoover rarely talked to newspapermen, and when he did, he insisted that their questions be written down and shown to him in advance. But on his fifth day in power, Roosevelt changed all that, calling

THE BRAIN TRUST

While running for president, Roosevelt didn't have time to study every national problem himself. One of his chief advisors, Sam Rosenman, suggested that Roosevelt put together a team of experts to offer him advice, saying, "My thought is that if we can get a small group together . . . they can prepare memoranda about such things as the relief of agriculture, tariffs, railroads, government debts, private credit, money, gold standard—all the things you will have to take a definite stand on." Following Rosenman's advice, Roosevelt surrounded himself with some of the

(continued)

ablest minds in the country. James Kieran of *The New York Times* called this diverse group of economists and professors "the brains trust." The press at large quickly shortened that to "brain trust."

At work Roosevelt was a leader who got the best out of his staff. "He is the best picker of brains who ever lived," one aide said. Indeed, in the early days of his presidency, Roosevelt sought suggestions from as many different advisors as he could. To the dismay of some, Roosevelt often gave the impression of agreeing with whomever he happened to be speaking to at the moment. But even those whose ideas he ultimately ruled against found it hard to hold a grudge. Jesse H. Jones was Roosevelt's secretary of commerce. Even after being fired, Jones said, "You just can't help liking that fellow."

the first of the record-breaking 998 press conferences he would hold while president. More than one hundred reporters gathered in the Oval Office. Perfectly at ease, Roosevelt answered question after question. The reporters were so charmed by his manner and pleasantly surprised by his remarkable candor that they gave him an ovation.

With the press on his side, Roosevelt then set out to win over the nation. On Sunday, March 12, eight days after assuming office, Roosevelt gave the first of many "fireside chats," or talks broadcast over the radio, to the American people. Part of Roosevelt's brilliance as a politician was his ability to break down complicated problems and explain them simply but without belittling listeners. His first subject was the nation's banking system.

My friends, I want to tell you what has been done in the last few days, why it was done, and what the next steps are going to be. . . . First of all, let me state the simple fact that when you deposit money in a bank the bank does not put the money into a safe-deposit vault. It invests your money in many different forms of credit.

Roosevelt's fireside chats, broadcast via radio, were his opportunity to explain the nation's issues to the American people in simple terms.

Roosevelt went on to explain to the country what protections had been put in place to guarantee the safety of their savings and why it was safer to put their money back into the bank than to keep it at home. The next morning Roosevelt's week-long strategy paid off. With renewed faith in the country's economic system, Americans lined up to put their money back in the nation's banks. It was a triumphant beginning to his term in office. Even Walter Lippmann, the journalist who had doubted Roosevelt's qualifications to be president, was impressed. "In one week," Lippmann wrote, "the nation, which had lost confidence in everything and everybody, has regained confidence in the government and in itself."

THE ONE HUNDRED DAYS

The passage of the Emergency Banking Relief Act marked the beginning of the most active legislative session in American history. With Americans looking to the White House to take action,

Customers wait in line to reinvest their money in an American bank.

Roosevelt created agency after agency, aimed at what he called the "three R's"—relief, recovery, and reform. For a period known as the Hundred Days, Congress rubber-stamped the president's programs into law. As he had done as assistant secretary of the navy, Roosevelt showed a great ability to improvise. He said, "It is common sense to take a method and try it. If it fails, admit it frankly and try another. But above all, try something." Roosevelt's agenda soon took shape as a host of agencies that came to be known by their initials.

The **Civilian Conservation Corps** (CCC) was born out of Roosevelt's idea to put unemployed men to work in the nation's forests. At first the labor secretary Frances Perkins (whom

Roosevelt had brought to the White House from his days in New York) commented, "Just because they're unemployed doesn't mean that they're natural-born lumbermen." When Roosevelt insisted, Perkins suggested that the program be administered by the army, which had plenty of trucks, tents, and other suitable equipment. The bill was passed into law on the last day of March 1933, and was the government's first full-fledged attempt at nationwide relief. Each worker, or corpsman, hired by the CCC received $1 a day, plus room and board. By mid-June, 239,644 men were enrolled and split into 1,330 work camps. These workers planted trees, fought forest fires, built lookout towers, and ran telephone lines. Overall the project was deemed a success. American men were given jobs; communities and forests were improved. By the time the agency was dissolved in 1942, because of World War II, 2.5 million men had worked in the corps.

Civilian Conservation Corps workers clear the way for a new road.

ROOSEVELT ON RACE

Throughout his presidency Roosevelt made sure that every New Deal program helped African Americans as well as whites. Even so he did not fight for broader laws guaranteeing all Americans their civil rights, fearing that the conservative southern Democrats whose support he needed to pass his New Deal legislation into law would vote against him if they felt he was fighting too vigorously for racial equality.

The CCC bylaws stated that "no discrimination shall be made on account of race, color, or creed." In reality CCC labor camps were segregated. Many southerners didn't want African-American CCC work groups in their states at all. Still, Roosevelt did what he could to promote blacks within the organization. In 1935 he authorized the promotion of thirty-nine African-American reserve officers. Two years later he wrote to the CCC director Robert Fechner, asking for more African-American chaplains: "I understand we have over two hundred camps for black boys but that there are only six black chaplains in these camps and only eleven medical officers. Can you increase this percentage?"

Later, in 1941, Roosevelt signed Executive Order 8802, which banned discrimination in the defense industry.

Other agencies were formed to put America's less fortunate to work. There were the Public Works Administration (PWA), the Civil Works Administration (CWA), and the Works Progress Administration (WPA). Although the CWA ended in 1934, the WPA and PWA provided federal relief until the early 1940s.

Opponents complained that a critical aspect of the American national character—the ability for each citizen to get through hard times unassisted—was being compromised. *Boondoggling* was the word opponents gave to describe WPA projects that they felt were a waste of money. But Roosevelt and his supporters pointed out that the men and women working for the WPA and other government programs weren't getting anything for free. Over its lifetime the WPA and other agencies employed 8 million Americans who worked—and worked hard. During Harry Hopkins's tenure as head of the WPA, workers built 10 percent of the new roads in the country, 35 percent of the new hospitals, and 65 percent of the new city halls. They built New York City's Lincoln Tunnel and the Triborough Bridge. They built the Washington, D.C., zoo; the Mall; the Federal Trade Commission; Kentucky's Fort Knox; and Colorado's Boulder (later Hoover) Dam. At the same time writers employed by the WPA wrote detailed tourist guidebooks to every state. Artists were given money to paint murals in public spaces. Actors put on plays in regions where people had never seen live theater.

In his first months in office, Roosevelt also sought to help the nation's farmers. For years huge food surpluses had resulted in farmers receiving low prices for their crops. On May 12, 1933,

A poster announces a New York City guide written by WPA workers.

THE TENNESSEE VALLEY AUTHORITY

The Tennessee River Basin covers 640,000 square miles and parts of seven states—Virginia, North Carolina, Tennessee, Georgia, Alabama, Mississippi, and Kentucky—and before the New Deal was known primarily for its horrible floods and crippling poverty. In some areas 30 percent of the people had malaria. Only 3 percent of the farms had electricity. Families lived on only cornmeal and salt pork.

On May 18, 1933, Congress created the Tennessee Valley Authority, or TVA—a government agency that, over time, built a series of dams and hydroelectric plants that controlled floods and brought electricity more widely to the region. Opponents objected to state planning of such magnitude. But to the people who benefited, the TVA was a positive example of good government planning.

Congress passed the **Agricultural Adjustment Act** (AAA). This law proposed to do something that seemed contrary to common sense: the government would pay farmers *not* to produce certain crops. With fewer crops on the market, demand rose, and farm prices shot up. But even though the AAA helped farmers maintain a higher standard of living, many consumers protested the higher food prices. And some Americans questioned a policy that compelled farmers to destroy food in times when so many people were going hungry. The secretary of agriculture Henry Wallace agreed: "I hope we shall never have to resort to it again," he said. "To destroy a standing crop goes against the soundest instincts of human nature."

During Roosevelt's second fireside chat, delivered on May 7, 1933, he said that he wanted to form "a partnership in planning" between the government and business. He wanted the government to have the right to "prevent, with the assistance of the overwhelming majority in that industry, unfair practices and to enforce this agreement by the authority of government." Roosevelt's idea took form as the **National Recovery Administration**, or NRA. Led by General Hugh Johnson, the NRA drew up codes for fair business practices and expected U.S. businesses to obey. The NRA gave workers the right to form unions and establish guidelines for maximum hours worked and a minimum wage. For the first time in American history, workers were guaranteed the right to collective bargaining. At the same time Johnson launched a nationwide campaign to get every American employer to agree to a $12, forty-hour workweek for employees. Businesses that agreed to follow the NRA codes were allowed to fly a symbolic blue eagle outside their doors. In Boston, Mayor James Curley led local children in a pledge: "I promise as a good American citizen to do my part for the NRA. I will buy only where the Blue Eagle flies. I will ask my family to buy . . . American-made goods."

Undoubtedly the NRA rallied the country around the idea of long-overdue labor reforms, many of which would be officially passed into law soon thereafter. But the NRA had too many codes to enforce. Detractors called it "creeping socialism" because the government was regulating businesses so heavily. Others said that *NRA* stood for "No Recovery Allowed." Worse, many businesses flying the blue eagle were found to be in violation of many NRA codes. Then, in 1935, the Supreme Court unanimously found that the NRA was unconstitutional, holding that Congress was not allowed to "delegate legislative powers" to the Executive Branch. Though Roosevelt was furious, the

A 1933 political cartoon by Clifford Berryman illustrates the cooperation between employees and employers who support the NRA.

Supreme Court helped him turn away from one of his programs that was garnering mixed results.

As Roosevelt looked toward a second term as president, he had reason to feel proud. The Federal Deposit Insurance Corporation (FDIC), created in 1933, was a governmental agency that insured bank deposits. In 1934 the Security and Exchange Commission, or SEC, was established to regulate the stock market. In 1935 Roosevelt signed the National Labor Relations Act (or Wagner Act), which gave workers the right to form unions. Also in 1935 Congress passed the **Social Security Act**, a law that created an automatic pension system for working Americans, funded by payroll taxes on employees and employers. Provisions were also made for blind, crippled, and delinquent children. Though attacked as too expensive or, once again, socialistic, Social Security has become a fixture of American life. Today every working American can be rest assured that, in retirement, he or she will have some sort of income.

A 1935 poster issued by the Social Security Board urges citizens to take advantage of the Social Security Act.

REELECTION

By 1936 Roosevelt's supporters had a lengthy list of accomplishments to point to. Corporate profits were rising, and new jobs had been created. Farming income was up, and hundreds of homes had been saved from foreclosure. On the other hand, the Depression hadn't gone away. Many Americans were still unemployed. But it wasn't the poor who disapproved of Roosevelt. Though he argued that his policies had saved American capitalism, the nation's rich decried New Deal policies that made it more difficult for corporations to do business. "During all the time I was gone," one Roosevelt-hater who was traveling in the Caribbean said, "if anybody asked me if I wanted any news, my reply was always— 'there is only one bit of news I want to hear and that is the death of Franklin D. Roosevelt.'" It was reported that a Connecticut country club forbade the mention of Roosevelt's name as a "health measure against apoplexy," or stroke.

In the end Roosevelt was reelected in 1936 over the mild Kansas governor Al Landon by a landslide. But headed into election season, the outcome was in question. After all, the Democrats had gained power before, under Grover Cleveland and Woodrow Wilson, only to lose it quickly. In 1935 the columnist Paul Mall wrote,

> *This is a Republican country; the Republicans alone can bring prosperity; . . . the voters merely chastise them occasionally, but always restore them to favor after a brief, unsatisfactory experience with the Democrats.*

At the 1936 Democratic convention, Roosevelt struck back, saying, "These economic royalists complain that we seek to overthrow the institutions of America. What they really complain of is that we seek to take away their power." Roosevelt went on, "Never before in all our history have these forces been so united against one candidate as they stand today. They are unanimous in their hate for me—and I welcome their hatred." Roosevelt made the campaign a **referendum** on himself. "There's one issue in this campaign," he said. "It's myself, and people must be either for me or against me."

When the votes were counted on election day, Roosevelt carried every state except Maine and Vermont, winning 523 electoral votes to Landon's 8. The Democrats won so many seats in Congress that they outnumbered Republicans by four

Roosevelt accepts the nomination for a second presidential term at the National Democratic Convention in Philadelphia in 1936.

to one. For many years there had been a saying in American politics: "As Maine goes, so goes the nation." Now Democrats joked, "As Maine goes, so goes Vermont." Someone suggested that Roosevelt balance the budget by selling the two states off to Canada.

In the end Roosevelt won for his championing of "the forgotten man." Poor Americans, ravaged by the Depression, were not going to vote against the man who had come to their rescue. As Al Smith of New York put it, no one "shoots at Santa Claus."

SECOND TERM AND RUMBLINGS OVERSEAS Five

$\mathcal{R}$oosevelt rightly interpreted the 1936 election results as a mandate to continue the policies of the New Deal. As senators and representatives adjourned in March of 1937, the Democratic Party controlled both houses of Congress by a whopping 75 percent. In some quarters there was talk that the Republican Party might not survive.

But poised for continued success, an overconfident Roosevelt began his second term with the biggest blunder of his presidency. Yes, the Democrats had controlled the presidency and both houses of Congress for four years. But the nation's third branch, the Supreme Court, was still in the hands of nine mostly elderly, conservative Republicans. These were the justices who had declared the NRA unconstitutional a year after its creation and then killed off the AAA, the Securities and Exchange Act, and many other New Deal programs. Furious, Roosevelt began his second term determined to change the makeup of the court.

ROOSEVELT "PACKS" THE COURT

According to the U.S. Constitution, Supreme Court justices are nominated by the president and confirmed by the Senate. Reelected by a landslide, Roosevelt decided to bring the full weight of his enormous popularity to bear on America's judicial system. In his view the people had spoken: they wanted the New Deal. To that end, the Supreme Court had to step into line.

Digging back through old court records, Roosevelt's attorney general, Homer S. Cummings, discovered a document from 1913. Ironically it had been written by then Attorney General James C. McReynolds, one of the most conservative members of the current court. The document spelled out a proposal to invigorate the court by adding one judge for every one who was over seventy years old. Soon Roosevelt sent his own version of the idea to Capitol Hill, arguing that the strain of handling the court's **docket** was too much for elderly judges. Accordingly a new judge should be added to the court for every justice over seventy.

In truth the size of the Supreme Court had been increased or decreased six previous times in history, usually at the request of the president. But the last time it had been done was in 1869, and in the intervening years a nine-judge court had become the virtual law of the land. While Republicans stood uniformly against Roosevelt's bill, many Democrats also objected to what they felt was an abuse of presidential power. The liberal senator Burton K. Wheeler said, "A liberal cause was never won by stacking a deck of cards, by stuffing a ballot box, or by packing a court." On March 22, 1937, the chief justice of the Supreme Court, Charles Evans Hughes, took the unprecedented step of submitting a statement on the subject to Congress. In it Hughes shot down Roosevelt's main rationale for packing the court. Having more judges, Hughes wrote, would slow down the workings of the court, not speed them up. There would be "more judges to hear, more judges to confer, more judges to discuss, more judges to be convinced and to decide."

Though public opinion turned against the president, Roosevelt refused to back down—even when the Supreme Court suddenly reversed its ruling against part of the NRA, deciding that

A political cartoon shows the Democratic donkey kicking in objection to Roosevelt's Supreme Court reform.

a state had the right to set a minimum wage for its workers. After that, the court began to back up New Deal policies that it had previously struck down as unconstitutional. When Congress voted full pay for justices over seventy who retired, one of the older jurists on the bench took the bait, allowing Roosevelt to make his first appointment, swinging the court even further to the left. Still, Roosevelt refused to drop the court bill. When it came up for a vote in Congress, it was soundly defeated.

The New Deal Stumbles

Roosevelt's court fight hurt him deeply. With his first major defeat in five years, Roosevelt angered conservative southern Democrats, who then began to vote Republican on subsequent New Deal legislation. Before the midterm elections of 1938, Roosevelt toured the country, campaigning for liberal candidates who would support his programs. But for the first time since he was elected, the Democrats lost seats in Congress. In the South some conservatives became Democrats only in name—a realignment that would hamper the party's ability to pass legislation for years to come. In 1962 the Democratic president John F. Kennedy observed, "Some Democrats have voted with Republicans for twenty-five years, really since 1938 . . . so that we have a very difficult time, on a controversial piece of legislation, securing a working majority."

During his first term, whatever Roosevelt proposed was passed into law. During his second term he had a harder time. Yes, the Supreme Court was finally approving of a host of New Deal legislation. But with Congress less willing to work with him, Roosevelt had trouble passing new laws. At the same time the late 1930s were marked by a sharp increase in labor unrest. The Wagner Act had given workers the right to strike and form unions. But many businesses did whatever they could to deny employees those rights. On Memorial Day, 1937, at the Republic Steel Plant in Chicago, striking workers fought with police. In Detroit Henry Ford hired his own thugs to intimidate would-be strikers. At the same time, while the worst days of the Depression were over, the nation underwent a recession that critics dubbed "the Roosevelt Depression."

Even so, Roosevelt enjoyed some domestic successes during his second term. The **Fair Labor Standards Act** set a nationwide minimum wage of $0.25 an hour, established a forty-hour workweek, and finally abolished child labor. But in truth, Roosevelt's attention had begun to turn to alarming events overseas. As early as 1935, Roosevelt had written a friend, "I still worry about world affairs more than domestic problems." As the decade marched on, Roosevelt had more and more to worry about.

CHAOS IN EUROPE

When Roosevelt was elected president, World War I had been over for a decade. But that didn't mean Americans had forgotten the 300,000 or more casualties it suffered. In less than two years of fighting, more than 50,000 Americans had been killed. And for what? Woodrow Wilson had promised that the Great War would be a "war to end wars." Instead the League of Nations he helped create was shunned by Americans looking inward, embracing Warren Harding's "Return to Normalcy." During the Roaring Twenties Americans distanced themselves from world events, focusing instead on getting rich and having fun. Former European allies were reviled by many Americans as countries that didn't repay their debts, as set out in the **Treaty of Versailles**.

But significant and frightening events were happening overseas. In the wake of the World War I, Germany's economy was in shambles. In 1924 a failed Austrian artist named Adolf Hitler wrote *Mein Kamp*, a book that laid out a plan for a united and thriving Germany based on the superiority of the white race. By the time the worldwide depression hit in the early 1930s, Hitler was the head of the German National Socialist Party, whose platform blamed Germany's economic woes on Jews, Marxists, and foreign powers. The same month that Franklin Roosevelt assumed office in 1933, Adolf Hitler declared himself Germany's dictator and, in open defiance of the Treaty of Versailles, began to rearm his country. In March of 1938 Germany conquered Austria. In September Hitler demanded and received the German Sudetenland, which had been incorporated into Czechoslovakia in 1918. With virtually no British or French resistance, Hitler took the rest of Czechoslovakia in early 1939, then attacked Poland that summer. On September 3 Britain and France declared war on Germany. But America's future allies were no match for the

Adolf Hitler, leader of the German National Socialist (Nazi) Party, is greeted with the Nazi salute.

now-powerful German army. By the summer of 1940 the Nazis controlled Denmark, Norway, the Netherlands, Belgium, and France. Only England remained free of its control.

Trouble was brewing in Italy and Japan as well. In 1925 Benito Mussolini, the son of a blacksmith, had installed himself as dictator of Italy. In the Far East in 1937 an increasingly militaristic Japan sank the U.S. gunboat *Panay* as it anchored peacefully in the Yangtze River. That same year Japan invaded China and conquered Peking. Together, Germany, Italy, and Japan formed the Axis Powers—the countries that the United States and its allies eventually fought in World War II.

FIGHTING NEUTRALITY

Roosevelt knew that to ignore the rise of Nazi Germany was to risk not only America's safety but also the future of worldwide democracy. Unfortunately few other Americans saw it that way. Though Roosevelt was eager to help American allies overseas, his hands were tied by the **Neutrality Act** of 1935, a law he regretted signing that forbade the U.S. government from selling arms to countries at war. In 1937, despite obvious German territorial ambitions and Japanese aggressiveness, Congress extended the Neutrality Act. *The New York Times* noted, "The passage of this . . . neutrality bill may mark the high tide of isolationist sentiment in this country." Nine months later Representative Louis Ludlow of Indiana introduced the Ludlow Resolution, which stated that a declaration of war by Congress could not take effect until confirmed by a majority of Americans in a nationwide referendum. Such a bill would have made it nearly impossible for any president to conduct foreign policy. Luckily cooler heads prevailed, and the resolution was defeated.

Summoning a country so committed to remaining neutral to fight was, perhaps, Roosevelt's greatest challenge. In 1940 America's army was the eighteenth strongest in the world, with only five ready-for-action divisions. In contrast, that same year, the Germans had launched an attack along the Western Front in Europe with 136 divisions. The historian Doris Kearns Goodwin explains America's predicament:

In the spring of 1940, the United States possessed almost no munitions industry at all. So strong had been the recoil from the war after 1918 that both the government and the private sector had backed away from making weapons. The result was that, while the

United States led the world in the mass production of automobiles, washing machines, and other household appliances, the techniques of producing weapons of war had badly atrophied.

Roosevelt did what he could to prepare the nation for the challenges ahead. In 1937 he gave a speech in Chicago in which he called for a **quarantine** of aggressor nations. But the press lashed out, accusing Roosevelt of warmongering. Isolationist congressmen threatened to begin impeachment proceedings. Roosevelt said wryly to a friend, "It's a horrible thing to look over your shoulder when you are trying to lead—and find no one there."

Still, Roosevelt didn't give up. Even the most hard-core isolationist understood the argument behind having a strong navy to

Workers assemble washing machines in a factory that once produced wartime aircraft.

An endless line of B-24 Liberators on the production line in Detroit, Michigan

protect American interests on the Atlantic Ocean against German boats and submarines. On January 28, 1938, Congress granted Roosevelt $2 billion to build a navy capable of patrolling both the Atlantic and Pacific oceans. But Roosevelt was convinced that the coming war would be won by airpower. In the late 1930s Germany was estimated to have 8,000 bombers and fighting planes, whereas the United States had only 1,650 pilots, several hundred planes, and thirteen B-17s on order, due to be delivered by the end of the year. Roosevelt gave the order to drastically expand the air force, a decision to which generals attributed the winning of the war years later.

War Comes to the United States

With France in the hands of the Germans and Britain fighting for its life, Roosevelt, recently reelected, came upon a way to help Britain more directly without officially joining the war. "Suppose my neighbor's home catches on fire," Roosevelt told the Washington press corps on December 17, 1940:

. . . If he can take my garden hose and connect it up with his hydrant, I may help him to put out his fire. Now, what do I do? I don't say to him before that operation, 'Neighbor, my garden hose cost me $15; you have to pay me $15 for it.' What is the transaction that goes on? I don't want $15—I want my garden hose back after the fire is over.

Thus Roosevelt described what came to be known as the Lend-Lease policy. From that point forward, the United States gave Britain whatever boats, planes, or munitions it needed. In return Britain simply had to promise to return in kind what it didn't use at the end of the war. With the exception of the hardline isolationists, Congress agreed overwhelmingly with Roosevelt's plan. With America's help, Britain hung on for dear life.

Roosevelt and his advisors were also concerned about Japanese territorial ambitions in the Far East. To that end Roosevelt loaned money to Chinese nationalists and banned the export of gasoline, iron, and oil to Japan. The United States demanded that Japan return all the territory it had taken by force. Led by General Hideki Tōjō, a war hawk, Japan refused.

Some historians believe that Roosevelt goaded Japan into attacking the United States to have the excuse he needed to jump

The First Three-Termer

As the 1930s drew to a close, Roosevelt claimed that he had no greater wish than to retire. But with troubles brewing in Europe and the Republican Party remaining steadfastly isolationist, Roosevelt eventually bowed to the pleas of his advisors and fellow Democrats and ran for an unprecedented third term. His opponent was the ex-Democrat, recently turned Republican businessman Wendell Wilkie. Wilkie did what he could to make Roosevelt's serving a third term an issue. He also accused Roosevelt of secretly wanting to lead the country into the European war.

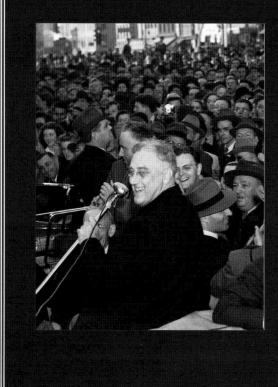

But Democrats cried, "Better a Third-Termer than a Third-Rater!" and Roosevelt won again. In the end Americans were wary of passing on the presidency to an unproven politician during the middle of an international crisis.

Eventually Roosevelt was elected to a fourth term as well. But in 1951, the Twenty-second Amendment to the Constitution was ratified, which limited the number of terms a president could serve to two.

into the war in Europe. Many historians, however, contend that a war with the Far East was inevitable. After all, Japan was a small island looking to control great amounts of territory. In any event, by early December of 1941, broken Japanese code told of a coming attack. Most Americans assumed that this meant an assault on the naval base in the Philippines. Few predicted that Japan had the military power or the will to strike U.S. soil. But on the morning of December 7, 1941, Japanese warplanes descended on America's

U.S. war ships burn in Pearl Harbor after a surprise attack by the Japanese.

naval base at Pearl Harbor in Hawaii. By the time the attack was over, 18 ships were sunk or seriously damaged, 200 airplanes were destroyed, and 2,403 people were killed.

The following morning a grim Roosevelt addressed the U.S. Congress:

> *Yesterday, December 7, 1941—a date which will live in infamy— the United States of America was suddenly and deliberately attacked by naval and air forces of the Empire of Japan. . . . No matter how long it may take us to overcome this premeditated invasion, the American people, in their righteous might, will win through to absolute victory.*

Franklin Roosevelt finally entered the nation into the war he had known all along that the United States had no choice but to fight to the finish.

The Japanese attack on Pearl Harbor sent shock waves through the American public. But in order to stop Germany from overrunning Britain, thereby seizing all of Europe, Roosevelt and his advisors opted for a war strategy that called for "getting Hitler first." Enough troops would be sent to the Far East to keep Japan contained, but the bulk of American forces would be sent to Europe.

Before a true mark on the war front could be made, the United States had to retool for military production. In August of 1941 Adolf Hitler dismissed the United States as a cowardly nation "whose conceptions of life are inspired by the most grasping commercialism." But Hitler greatly underestimated the American spirit. In the wake of the attack on Pearl Harbor, the U.S. economy moved quickly from a peace to a war footing.

But would it move quickly enough? Could the nation produce enough tanks, planes, guns, uniforms, boots, and the hundreds of other supplies needed to wage a war before Germany overran Europe? Yes, the nation had great industrial capacity, but as late as 1940, the country had so few rifles that troops in training sometimes practiced with broomsticks. With so much ground to make up, Roosevelt called for American businesses to reach seemingly impossible production targets. The War Production Board ordered U.S. companies to halt all nonessential building and to conserve materials for the war. As American men went overseas to fight, women and older men made up for the resulting labor shortage. To help fund the war

Women work at the American Can Company in Forest Park, Georgia, assembling borne torpedoes.

effort—in the end the total bill was upward of $330 billion—the government raised money by selling war bonds, redeemable in the future by the U.S. Treasury. At the same time Americans rationed everything from sugar, butter, and rubber to lawn mowers, waffle irons, birdcages, and electric trains. Everything went to the war effort. The results were remarkable. In the five years after the fall of France, American factories churned out 296,429 warplanes, 102,351 tanks, 87,620 war ships, and 44 billion rounds of ammunition. As Roosevelt once said, "Oh, the production people can do if they really try!"

On the Battlefield

Unfortunately the nation's impressive retooling for war didn't translate into early victories on the battlefield. In the year following Pearl Harbor, American troops suffered defeat after defeat. Moving quickly Japan launched successful attacks on American outposts in Guam, Wake, and the Philippines, and also seized Hong Kong and British Malaya—a critical supplier of rubber. The Japanese also took control of the famed Burma Road, the route the United States had used to supply Chinese nationalists.

A Japanese cruiser after being attacked by U.S. planes during the Battle of Midway.

Though American troops fought valiantly on the Bataan Peninsula in the Philippines, General Douglas MacArthur eventually had to pull back, saying famously, "I shall return." The captured American and Filipino prisoners of war were forced to march 55 miles in the so-called Bataan death march. As many as ten thousand soldiers perished. Not until May of 1942 did American forces check the Japanese military, defending Australia by winning a battle in the Coral Sea. Then, in early June, the U.S. navy won the Battle of Midway, stopping the Japanese from gaining a strategic base from which they could have launched new attacks on the Hawaiian Islands.

Internment Camps

It began the morning after Pearl Harbor. California authorities dismissed Japanese Americans (issei, first-generation Americans, and nisei, children of issei), many of whom were U.S. citizens, from civil service jobs and revoked the licenses of Japanese Americans to practice law and medicine. Soon insurance companies were canceling Japanese-American policies. Milkmen refused to deliver milk to them; stores wouldn't sell them groceries. Signs in barbershops read, "JAPS SHAVED. NOT RESPONSIBLE FOR ACCIDENTS."

February 19, 1942, saw Franklin Roosevelt's worst hour as president. He signed Executive Order 9066, which authorized the War Department to establish "military areas" to which Japanese and Japanese-American civilians who lived with 60 miles of the West Coast could be relocated. The states of California and Arizona used the order to intern—in effect, jail—Japanese Americans. On March 27 issei and nisei were given forty-eight hours to dispose of their homes and businesses. Upward of 125,000 Japanese Americans were interned in "relocation centers" that were not much better than concentration camps, where families lived six or seven to a small room, with no stove or running water. These camps were often located far from the coast, keeping the would-be traitors from the U.S. shore that faced Japan. Still, at the end of the war, when the internment camps were shut down, the issei and nisei found that they could not get back their rightful property. It was not until 1990 that surviving internees received an official apology and reparation.

In Europe, American forces also started slowly. In the early part of the war German U-boats, or submarines, downed American merchant ships. Slowly, air patrol, radar, and depth charges from destroyers muted the German attacks. On the ground the British general Bernard Montgomery drove back German troops from the Suez Canal in North Africa. In Russia the Red Army stopped the Germans at Stalingrad.

In January 1943 Roosevelt left the country to meet British Prime Minister Winston Churchill in Casablanca. There the two leaders announced that the only acceptable condition for ending

The Big Three—Stalin, Roosevelt, and Churchill—meet for a three-day conference to discuss plans to defeat Hitler.

the war would be the unconditional surrender of Germany. Later that year Roosevelt and Churchill met in Tehran, the capital of Iran, with the Russian premier Joseph Stalin. The "Big Three" discussed the proposed Allied invasion of Europe—the second front of the war that Stalin had demanded for years. At the same time Roosevelt began to plan for the postwar world. He favored the creation of an international body, much like Woodrow Wilson's League of Nations, to **arbitrate** international disputes and keep the peace. In the fall of 1943 the Senate voted on the question, "Should the Senate resolve its willingness to join in establishing an international authority to preserve peace?" The

THE FINAL SOLUTION

In 1942 news of the Nazi concentration and death camps began to filter out of Europe. Sadly the reports that millions of Jews and other "undesirables" were being systematically put to death seemed too incredible to be believed. Even in wartime, how could a nation be so cruel?

In truth Adolf Hitler and his Third Reich had been planning these actions for a decade. In the 1930s Nazi Germany passed laws that deprived Jewish citizens of basic civil rights. As the war got under way, Germany erected giant concentration camps to take advantage

(continued)

of the slave labor of Jewish men and women. By 1941 Jews from all over conquered Europe were sent by train to death camps for what came to be known as the Final Solution—their plan to exterminate the Jewish people.

Tragically, even after the reports of mass graves were confirmed, Allied commanders refused to help stop the transport of victims to the camps. They argued that conducting bombing runs against the rail lines that led to the camps would divert planes that could be put to better use ending the war elsewhere.

Only when the fighting was over was the totality of one of the most unspeakable tragedies in human history fully discovered. Over the course of the war Nazi Germany had systematically killed 6 million Jews. Coupled with the murders of Soviet prisoners of war, Catholics, Slavs, homosexuals, and other so-called undesirables, the Nazis put approximately nine to eleven million people to death.

vote was a walloping 85 yes to 5 no, with 6 absent. After the experience of World War II, most Americans accepted that they could no longer isolate themselves from foreign affairs.

As the Allies gained the upper hand, General Dwight D. Eisenhower planned the largest assault of the war. On June 6, 1944—forever remembered as D-Day—Allied forces landed on the beaches of Normandy, France. Withstanding brutal German artillery fire, Allied forces stayed their ground and eventually marched all the way to Paris, liberating France after four years of German occupation. In October 1944 the first German city, Aachen, fell to the Americans. Victory was in sight.

American troops arrive on the Normandy coast in France on June 6, 1944, D-Day.

A Fourth Term and Yalta

In the fall of 1944 America's attention was on events overseas. But despite some talk of suspending the normal institutions of democracy "for the duration," another presidential election was fast approaching. Meeting that year in Chicago, the Republicans nominated the liberal New York governor Thomas E. Dewey to run. As for the Democrats, Roosevelt was the only choice. After all, how could the party—let alone the country—even consider changing leaders with the war on the brink of being won? Though Roosevelt was willing to serve, his health was clearly failing. He looked thin and drawn. Dark circles had taken up permanent residence under his eyes. To show that he was up to the task of leading the nation

Roosevelt on his birthday, January 29, 1944. The worries of the presidency had aged him considerably.

to ultimate victory and building a lasting peace, Roosevelt took to the campaign trail. Feeding off the energy of the crowds, Roosevelt seemed to revive. He was reelected, winning 432 electoral votes to Dewey's 99. Thrilled, he smiled at reporters and said, "The first twelve years are the hardest!"

By February 1945 the war in Europe was moving rapidly toward its final hours. Allied forces defeated Hitler's armies at the Battle of the Bulge, while the Soviets stormed into Hungary and Poland. The Far East, however, was another story. Though Japan was on the defensive, the empire was hardly defeated. The Pacific War was still raging.

That same month the "Big Three"—Roosevelt, Churchill, and Stalin—met in Yalta, a czarist palace on the Black Sea, to discuss the future of Europe after the war. Roosevelt came to the meeting with definite goals, among them to form a more effective version of the League of Nations and to figure out the fate of Poland. Most important, he also wanted Stalin's assurance that Russia would join the war against Japan. Generals told Roosevelt that the cost of a full-scale invasion of mainland Japan might cost one million casualties in American forces alone. By that point the United States was well on its way to developing the first atomic bomb, but it was a weapon that hadn't yet been tested.

With America and Britain desperate for Russian help on the battlefield, Stalin had the upper hand. In return for his commitment to take on the Japanese, Stalin demanded that the Soviets be given control of Manchuria and Mongolia. He also asked that a veto be given to major nations in the United Nations, and that the Soviet Union be one of them, along with the United States, Britain, France, and China. Though Stalin agreed that Poland should have a representative government, it didn't take him long to go back on his word.

Roosevelt's detractors felt that the "dying man" had failed at Yalta by allowing Stalin to take over all of Eastern Europe. But the truth is much fuzzier. As World War II was drawing to a bloody conclusion, Winston Churchill had urged the U.S. general Dwight Eisenhower to occupy as much of Eastern Europe as he could. But Eisenhower had pulled back his troops, which allowed Stalin to take control of Czechoslovakia and eastern Germany. With so much land already ceded to the Soviets, many historians believe it is unlikely that anything could have been done to stop the Soviet Union from taking control of Eastern Europe and contributing to the ensuing cold war.

Roosevelt's Legacy

On April 12, 1945, Roosevelt was vacationing in Warm Springs when he suffered a massive cerebral hemorrhage. He died later that day, leaving the country stunned. His voice shaking with emotion, Republican Robert A. Taft, Roosevelt's archrival, said, "He dies a hero of the war, for he literally worked himself to death in the service of the American people." Around the country and around the world, people expressed their shock and sorrow as Vice President Harry S. Truman took the oath of office. A few months later it was Truman who gave the order to

THE FIRST LADY

Eleanor Roosevelt was the most politically involved, effective First Lady in history. A woman with great passion for the underdog, Eleanor became the loudest voice of outspoken liberalism in her husband's administrations. Of all his advisors, she was perhaps the one he valued most, as she traveled the country and reported back on what she saw. "I realized," she once said in a radio interview, "that if I remained in the White House all the time I would lose touch with the rest of the world."

During World War II Eleanor was instrumental in the issuance of directives that desegregated government-owned recreational areas and buses. A tireless labor advocate, she made sure that American workers were treated fairly. As the war drew to a close, Eleanor pushed her husband to support a G.I. bill of rights that would give returning veterans money to go to college. After her husband's death,

Eleanor stayed in the public eye as the U.S. representative to the United Nations. Year after year, women across the country voted her the most popular woman in America. At age seventy-four she wrote, "We must regain a vision of ourselves as leaders of the world. We must join in an effort to use all knowledge for the good of all human beings. When we do that, we shall have nothing to fear."

Eleanor Roosevelt died on November 7, 1962, and was buried next to her husband at Hyde Park.

drop two atomic bombs on Japan, finally bringing World War II to a close.

Today Roosevelt is remembered, along with George Washington and Abraham Lincoln, as one of America's three great presidents. Like any human being, he made mistakes. In the flush of a landslide reelection, he tried to pack the Supreme Court. He allowed Japanese Americans to be robbed of their civil rights and interred. But Roosevelt's positives far outweigh his negatives. Though largely despised by the wealthy of his era, it can be safely said that Roosevelt was capitalism's savior, restoring confidence in America's banks and businesses at a time when many Americans were at the end of their collective ropes. An awe-inspiring array of the laws passed during the New Deal years are still on the books today, ensuring that the American workplace is fairer and safer. The success of Social Security alone would be legacy enough for most presidents. And then there was Roosevelt's foresight in recognizing the looming threat in Europe and his wise, unwavering wartime leadership. On the eve of the millennium, the Pulitzer Prize–winning historian Arthur Schlesinger Jr. wrote,

Take a look at our present world. It is manifestly not Adolf Hitler's world. His Thousand-Year Reich turned out to have a brief and bloody run of a dozen years. It is manifestly not Joseph Stalin's world. That ghastly world self-destructed before our eyes. Nor is it Winston Churchill's world. Empire and its glories have long since vanished into history.

The world we live in today is Franklin Roosevelt's world. Of the figures who for good or evil dominated the planet 60 years ago, he would be least surprised by the shape of things at the millennium. And confident as he was of the power and vitality of democracy, he would welcome the challenges posed by the century to come.

Franklin Delano Roosevelt was elected during the Great Depression. He led his country through economic recovery, instituting his New Deal, and leading the nation through World War II. He is the only U.S. president to be elected for four consecutive terms.

1882
Born in Hyde Park,
New York

1904
Graduates from Harvard
University

1905
Marries fifth cousin Eleanor
Roosevelt

1910
Elected state senator in
New York

1913
Named assistant secretary
of the navy

1920
Nominated vice president of
the United States

1921
Contracts polio

1880

1928
Elected governor of
New York

1932
Elected president of the
United States

1933
Introduces the New Deal

1936
Reelected president of the
United States

1940
Reelected to a third term
as president of the United
States

1944
Reelected to an unprece-
dented fourth term as
president of the United
States

1945
Dies on April 12 in Warm
Springs

1950

Agricultural Adjustment Act (AAA) law passed in 1933 to regulate farm output and prices

arbitrate the act of settling a dispute

Civilian Conservation Corps (CCC) program created in 1933 that put unemployed Americans to work on government projects

civil rights the rights of personal liberty (guaranteed to all people in the United States by the Constitution)

constituents the people a politician represents

Democrat America's political party that favors using government programs to help its citizens

docket a list of legal cases to be tried

Electoral College the body that elects the president and vice president of the United States

Emergency Banking Relief Act law passed in 1933 to reform America's banking system

executive power the power granted to (or taken by) the president

Fair Labor Standards Act law passed in 1938 that set a nationwide minimum wage and a forty-hour workweek, and abolished child labor

income tax a yearly tax on a person's earnings

League of Nations body set up after World War I to settle international disputes

National Recovery Administration (NRA) the New Deal organization that drew up fair competition codes for businesses

Neutrality Act the law in 1935 that forbade the U.S. government from selling arms to countries at war

polio an acute infectious disease caused by the poliovirus that, in extreme cases, can lead to paralysis

quarantine a state of enforced isolation

referendum a vote on an issue

Republican America's political party that generally favors a smaller federal government

Social Security Act law passed in 1935 that created the program that provides benefits to America's elderly and disabled

sweatshop slang term for an overcrowded, unsafe factory

Tammany Hall corrupt New York political organization that was powerful in the nineteenth and twentieth centuries

Treaty of Versailles peace treaty signed in 1919 that officially ended World War I

United Nations body founded in 1945 to replace the League of Nations to give aid and arbitrate international disputes

Books

Bardhan-Quallen, Sudipta. *Franklin Delano Roosevelt: A National Hero.* New York: Sterling, 2007.

Caplan, Jeremy. *Time for Kids: Franklin D. Roosevelt: A Leader in Troubled Times.* New York: Harper Trophy, 2005.

Feinberg, Barbara Silberdick. *Franklin Roosevelt, America's 32nd President.* Danbury, CT: Children's Press, 2005.

Web Sites

American Heritage Center Museum
www.fdrheritage.org
This site explores the "cultural, historical, and other learning opportunities" on the life of Franklin Delano Roosevelt.

Franklin D. Roosevelt
www.whitehouse.gov/history/presidents/fr32.html
This site offers a brief biography of Franklin Delano Roosevelt and includes links to biographies of other presidents, as well as biographies and quizzes aimed at kids.

F.D.R. Presidential Library and Museum
www.fdrlibrary.marist.edu
This is a Web site devoted to the Franklin Delano Roosevelt Library, located in Hyde Park, New York. Historical papers, books, and personal items can be viewed there.

Bailey, Thomas A. *The American Pageant, A History of the Republic, Vols. 1 & 2, Fifth Edition*. Lexington, MA: D.C. Heath and Company, 1975.

Davis, Kenneth. *Don't Know Much About History*. New York: Crown Publishers, 1990.

Goodwin, Doris Kearns. *No Ordinary Time*. New York: Simon and Schuster, 1994.

Manchester, William. *The Glory and the Dream*. New York: Bantam, 1984.

Morgan, Ted. *F.D.R., a Biography*. New York: Simon and Schuster, 1985.

Perkins, Dexter. *The New Age of Franklin Roosevelt*. Chicago: The University of Chicago Press, 1957.

ABOUT THE AUTHOR

Dan Elish is the author of numerous books for children, including *The Trail of Tears*, *Vermont*, *Theodore Roosevelt*, and *James Madison*, for Benchmark Books. He lives in New York City with his wife and two children.